To My Second Love

by Petra Mourany

A poetic journey of love, pain, and loss of innocence

Copyright © 2022 Petra Mourany

All rights reserved. No part of this book may be reproduced or used in any manner without written permission of the copyright owner except for the use of quotations in a book review. For more information: *www.petramourany.com*

Editing: Clelia Lewis
Design: Margherita Buzzi
Typeset in Garaldo, Book and Italic
Cover: Roberta Zeta

First paperback edition February 2022
ISBN: 979-8-9857578-0-4

CONTENTS

9	Chains
10	Thief
12	Desert
13	Affection
14	Why so silly?
15	Quand?
16	Sewing
17	Fault
20	Aftermath
21	Red Pillow
22	You Can See Why
23	Mercedes to Malibu
24	String
25	Rien
26	Strange Love
27	Musician
28	Words
29	Cat
30	Glasses and Realizations
31	Mirages of the Mind
32	The Letter
34	Karaoke
35	Farewell
36	Which One?
37	Timing
38	Wings
39	Enough
40	Apple and the Tree

41	Not I
43	Mirror
44	Wise
45	Whore
46	All Shots Fired
47	Burn
48	Laura
49	Quel Dommage
50	When I Look At You
51	Ghosts
52	Everything or Nothing?
53	#1
54	#2
55	#3
56	Hunter and the Prey
57	Title-less
58	Wishes Come True
59	Who?
60	Let Go
61	White Walls
62	Crazy
63	On Second Thought
64	Demona
65	Broken Fairytale
66	Fall
67	Copy and Repeat
68	No Shame
69	Shadows
70	Emancipation
71	Confession
72	Dreams

73	Machine-Man
74	Toxic
75	Shush
76	Can't Tell
77	Blame
78	Turning Tables
79	Take Me Dancing
80	Pop Rock Shrimp
81	Flowing Words from a Torn Rose
84	Little Girl
85	Prize for Rotten Judgement
87	Une Mort Très Douce
88	At Last, A Poem to the Highest Caliber of Man
92	Seduced by the Devil
93	And For God's Sake, Walk Her to Her Car
96	Absolutes
98	Wolf in Sheep's Clothing
99	Question
100	From Comrade to Foe
101	Karma is a Poet
102	Enough Crying
103	Mea Culpa
104	Regaining Innocence: The Only Truth

FOREWORD

This book takes as its premise that there are three archetypes of love one might experience throughout life.

The first archetype is that of the First Love. This love is spontaneous, your heart is innocent and naïve, pure but shortsighted. From this love, you learn what you love about love. The first love is easy, filling your life with light and goodness, until it ends, often when each grows into their own.

The Third Love is a mature love. The love that makes you believe in love again; the love that feels different from all other loves. It not only feels safe but is safe. It's easy like the first, but it's grounded in truth, healing, and realism; it's built on a feeling of home instead of a feeling of false dreams. The Third Love is the love that makes you second-guess whether you were ever in love before.

Sandwiched between these two, comes the Second Love.

The Second Love is the dramatic love. The love that comes with unparalleled pain. The love of too many lessons; power plays, ups and downs, highs and lows, pushing and pulling. It is often a journey of loss of innocence, but also of growth and healing, because that is exactly what it forces you through. It changes you. It shows you a side of love that you may hate. You either grow from it or allow it to pull you further down. Though it is neither healthy nor sustainable, it is a kind of 'love' nonetheless. Above all else, the Second Love catalyzes a journey that teaches you so much about yourself.

A Second Love is not limited to one person. Second Loves can come in the form of many different people and repeat until you learn the lessons that you need to learn. In some cases, one person on their own journey of growth can represent more than one of these archetypes as they change into different people; they can start as your first, then grow into your second; or start as your second, then disappear for a decade and come back emerging as your third.

To My Second Love is a collection of poetry dedicated to the varied forms and faces belonging to the Second Love archetype and to this emotional journey of growth. It is a poetic journey inspired by real pain and real loves, exploring innocence lost as one grows beyond the archetypal "first love," before the archetypal "third love" enters someone's life. It explores lessons related to themes such as pain, sex, consent, trauma inner-child wounding, self-worth, and, most importantly, healing and love.

Chains

Being in love is being bound by chains
Invisible, yet stronger than iron
Your mind is no longer your own
Your heart is no longer your own
Your eyesight is fine
Yet your vision is blurred
Your thoughts remain coherent
Yet they are not sound

Granted will you be of freedom
Only when those chains are broken
But, broken too
Shall be your heart

Thief

I opened the door
To a robber thieving the house
I took them to my bedroom
I gave them all I had to lose

The robber took and took
Left without a thank you
But the door only closed halfway behind them
It neither shut nor locked
Too naïve was I, I left it so

The robber returned
I heard the door creak as it opened
But once again, my instincts I did not heed
The robber knew from where to take
For I was the one who once showed the way

They had already taken so much,
What harm if they took more?
The robber needs what I can give, said I
I could help them; show them hope again
The coat on my back would keep them warm
The food in my cabinets would fill their stomach
The pillows on my bed would bring them sleep at night
The shoes I chose would protect their feet on the path ahead
One day, maybe, they'd have enough to be the one to give

But a thief is a thief and cannot give
They took until there was no more to take
And wordless, left my house barren

I closed the door.

What they took was intangible
It can't be touched, seen, or smelt
But after a while, its absence is disastrously felt

Now my door stays locked
The deadbolt turned
The chain up

It is much colder in an empty house
Too cold that I worry
My limbs will lack the warmth
To open the door again
If on the other side may knock
Someone who came to give

Desert

When I loved love
So sad I believed it to be
That time, like wind erasing footprints on desert sands
Would slowly take the memories from me

Now, I would give much
To hold in my hands a rake
And smudge out the footprints
That linger in the dunes of my mind

Affection

It wasn't the sex
that made me fall in love with you
Nor a hand-to-hand touch
A peck on my cheek, hello
A kiss on my lips, goodbye
Symbols of affection
Which you so feared
And so often denied me

It was your smile, your mind, your heart
The excitement that lit your face
When you spoke about something you loved
The eagerness at the drop of a hat
To help anyone in need
Your eyes, the way they gleamed
At times when I would do things
That made you smile
Your calm, your cool, your logic
How safe and easy it was with you

That heart, damaged as it is
Cold, as people see it,
Is a diamond in the rough
Hardened, dusty, broken, concealed
I know it for what it really is
And that is why I loved you

You see, I know you held back
In part to protect me from this pain, but
You could've kissed me goodbye all those times
Held my hand when it felt right
It would not have worsened the blow,
Only lessened the damage
You left behind

Why so silly?

So many potential men
Too little time
To be taken out by all
And wined and dined

So many handsome smiles
Bright eyes that shine
Yet the eyes I wish for the most
Are not the ones that wish they were mine

Quand?

When will I learn
The art of being selfish?

Sewing

When a heart breaks
A needle and thread sew it back together
But even when whole again, it's not the same
The seams will forever linger, it's forever changed
Again, it will tear, a different way each time
And again, needle and thread stitch it back together
So that a person who has given their love in life
Will have a quilt of a heart
marked by a healed patchwork of loss

Fault

I said no
Very clear
I said no
Loud enough to hear

I said no
But you did not stop
I repeated no
But you climbed on top

Is it because I said it nicely?
Is it because I did not scream?
I told myself lay back
To put an end to this dream

You knew I didn't want to
When you put a hand to my neck
But I froze in quiet
Too shocked to object

Was the fault on me?
It was I after all
That found you
handsome to see
So charming and tall

I kissed you freely
I allowed you in
When you asked to enter
I thought I could trust you
Like I trusted him

The one I loved
Would have stopped
When I said no
But you did not

When I said the couch, he would've stayed
When I said "don't touch me there please"
He would've obeyed
When I said I don't want to have sex
He would've heard
But you chose not to listen
Yet I'm the one that's absurd?

The next day you went to kiss me
I turned my cheek
I felt cold
My body weak

I let you out
Why so empty I felt?
I went to my friend
And what a blow she dealt

You shouldn't have slept with him
The first words from her mouth
But I didn't want to
I wanted to shout
I told him no, I said instead
Well maybe he was drunk
And she shook her head
He's a nice guy
She began to insist
But don't nice guys listen
When you resist?

She saw my face
"He'll text tonight"
As if that offered me grace

But the lie she weaved stayed in my head
It was my fault, it happened in my bed
It was my fault, I wore that dress
It was my fault, I let his hand slip to my chest

You texted me indeed
But I did not reply
I felt so dirty
And began to cry

I went to bed wondering what I had done
See the blame shifted to where you had none
I heard my friend's words, so I was to blame
I texted you back to reclaim my name

And so began the pretense
Between my rapist and I
A strange obsession grew the lie
If we ended up together
At least it would mean
I was not raped
Nor a slut like it seemed

Aftermath

Crying in a bed
Cold and alone
Wishing you'd come and hug me
And whisper "you're home."

Red Pillow

I remember how when I tapped him a certain way
He would wrap his arms around me
And I would sleep on his arm like it was my pillow.
To know that I still have to see him every day
And wonder if after we say goodbye and go our separate ways
Someone else will be wrapped in those same arms
While some nights, without even realizing it, when I close my eyes
I still imagine it's his strong arm that my head is resting on
And not my soft red pillow.

You Can See Why

What do I do when I want comfort
But there's no one home
No one next door
Nor in the neighborhood nearby
Nor in the city an hour away
Not in the whole country
No one safe enough to hear my cry

You may ask why she made those decisions
Perhaps you don't see she was broken inside
Her soul cracked, with no one around to fix it
Her wound festering with the blame she wrongly pointed her own way
Innocence defiled by those tainted
And all of it disguised so well behind a smile
That knew too well how to hide

When the boat is too far to see with your naked eye
And the body is broken
When the nearest safety is a piece of rotting wood
Then I think you can see why

Mercedes to Malibu

Under the shimmering stars
In the night sky
I asked you how many you'd brought here
Told you not to lie

The ocean swayed below us
You held my face in your hands
"What cynicism caused you to ask this?
Don't ruin our chance"

In that second, I dropped all barriers
Let your wisdom ring through me
Lost my worries to your kisses
Let the flowers you gave me fall to the sea

Our chance was ruined regardless
And I take the full blame
I let my old lover in
I let my wounds play me back into his game

String

There's a tug
Like a string between two hearts

I've tried to cut it with scissors
But it seems invincible
I tried to use time on it
But it stayed
I tried distance
Both literal and in action
Both failed

So magical is this string
Untouchable by all
Is it a harness of safety?
Or a rope that's bound me
Entangled for eternity?

Rien

Nothing leaves you colder than
Holding on to hands that don't hold on to you

Strange Love

To my second love:
I loved you more than the first
But the love was not fast, not instant
Not a fairytale, not euphoric
Which made it more real
More honest
More painful when you went away
It lingered longer
It never felt like you were made for me, but I loved you
I was complete without you, but I loved you
I didn't like the way you made me feel sometimes, but I loved you
No false hopes, no façade, no fantasy, but I loved you
No romantic dinners, expensive gifts, beautiful words, but I loved you
You.
Not an idea of you in my head
Not dreams and fantasies, but you. As a person. In the present.
Your flaws, your highs, your lows, your weaknesses,
Your dreams, your smile, your laugh. I loved you.
So much so that it took me a while to realize it was love.
I will love my third more than you.
Because after you, it would take
More than a Trojan horse to pass through the
Repaved walls of my heart

Musician

You plucked the strings of my heart like a seasoned harpist.

Words

The saying is
"Words will never hurt you"
A lie
Not only do words hurt
But they heal
Words in the hands of some
Are the deadliest of blades
And in the hands of others
Are warmer than the warmest blanket
Comforting one's soul
Healing one's mind
Words are the beginning of existence
Words are the tool of creation
Be careful how you wield your words
And do not hold them back
If giving them, though hard for you
May warm the heart of another

Cat

It wasn't he who ruined the friendship.
It was you.

Glasses and Realizations

Sitting here on this cold plane
I realize that often
I feel more sober when I'm drunk.
When I look in the mirror
With my blood-alcohol level a bit high
I see something so different than when it's zero
Yet I, myself, am the same.
From the first glass of wine to the third
My thighs did not tone
My stomach did not shrink
My upper lip did not miraculously grow.
The wine in my bloodstream
Is like a shield
That silences all the doubts
The fear
The voices of past pains
That were not caused by myself
But have turned against me and linger still
Like a ghost haunting me
Blocking my eyes, my spirit, my mind
From seeing, knowing, feeling what's there.
I think clearly without fear,
I breathe easier
I look in the mirror and I recognize myself
The woman who hides from the voices
The woman who lives within
Me

Mirages of the Mind

The truth revealed in your eyes
Every time they meet my own
Says something different from that of your mouth
That I begin to wonder if it was my mind alone
That felt it all

The Letter

Dear _____,
Your eyes are as bright as your mind,
Your soul is as gold as your heart
I know in your own strange way, that you love me as well.
If I have lived a life tenfold easier than yours
And I am the way I am with you
Then I marvel that you still manage to be
The way you are with me
Cold as it sometimes is
But deep down, I know better
I know the waves and tides of emotion that brew in your heart
The storms of fear, doubt, inadequacy, pain
That cloud your mind and stop you frozen in your tracks
I see them all. The contradiction
The tug when you pull me closer to you
The hesitation which used to stop you in your tracks
And I've seen how you challenge this in yourself
For me

I care about you more than I understand
Sometimes when it hits me,
I don't know where it comes from or how it happened
But I know it's real. I say this without shame
In my eyes, you will always be worthy of this love
Although you swing my heart left to right
Cause it so much confusion
But after everything, after distance, time,
Pain, distractions, healing... everything
I am still so happy in your presence
Safe and warm in your arms
Understood without speaking
Cared about in a way I know is concrete

And although I know it's not a
Fairytale you hear about, or a blinding bomb
Of maddening, infatuated chemistry
I know it is love, simple and pure.
And it has proved to me that it doesn't fade
Its potency only grows weaker
Its calling only quieted by sober minds and distractions.

And my heart will break the day you leave
Even though my sober self will not acknowledge it.

Karaoke

The karaoke bar is where you sat
Sipping your drink as you watched me dance
I saw a friend come sit at the bar too
Later she'll tell me what she told you:

"Why don't you tell her?"
"What good would that do?"
"It would make her happy"
"No, it will multiply her pain by two"

You rose and went to the stage
Hoping that a mic and a love song
Would your tender feelings assuage
Standing next to me in a memory of bliss
You finished with a magnificent crescendo of a kiss

Was that supposed to help me understand?

So many told me they saw deep love in your eyes
As you watched me with a gleam
But with you saying nothing, it sounded like lies
Like a meaningless movie scene

What did it matter coming from everyone else
That one thing, you could not give?
My heart yearned to hear it from you, and now
I'll never know what in your heart truly lives

Farewell

I'm happy you left
Although I'm sad you're gone.
The two feelings twirl around one another
Like dancers that sway in time, not knowing
They each move in a different design.
The way you were before you left,
Those memories make my heart glow
Healing the wounds inflicted in the past
Cleaning the tarnished memory of you.
But I know had you stayed,
it would not have remained that way.
Yes, I love you still, but I'm glad you left.
My heart shattered when you turned to leave
But it began to mend with every step you took away

Which One?

I realized then
That I'm crying for myself
Because I spent so much time
Crying for a man
Who doesn't care for me
Although I refused to admit it
And this whole time
I thought I was crying
Only because I missed you

Timing

Could you smell
Could you sense
Did you dream
Did someone tell

Did you know
From so far away
I had someone new

Is that why
You waited until now
To come and tell me
What I meant to you
Suddenly you want me to see
To know and to hear
You profess your love
Loud and clear
Despite the fact
You're too far away
And nothing can come from this

It's like you knew.
As if you wanted me
While I was lying next to him
To be thinking of you

Wings

I come to the house and the little girl starts to cry
My wings are cut, I cannot fly
My old protector berates and demeans
I must hold my tongue at the attack of his screams.

Oh lover, please come take me away
I know you don't love me, but I'll forget that today
Suddenly you seem safer, more complete than before
I'll exchange lovemaking to be called a whore

To lie in your arms and forget what I left
And convince myself I am yours to protect
The lie grows and grows so I don't need to weep
These arms are home now, I can finally sleep.

I keep lying to myself and I bring you home
Knowing though a lie,
I won't walk into the battle alone.

Enough

Please stop,
I can't hear her name
I was thinking I love you,
Why'd you say it again?

You gave her everything
You've said it before
You give me nothing
What am I? Your whore?

Everything and nothing
Don't mean to me
Dollars and dinners
And countries to see

You gave her yourself
And absolutes
You gave her acknowledgement
You set up roots

Don't tell me about the cathedral in Istanbul
Or the capital of Bulgaria—my ears are full
I don't want to hear about Modern Family
Or Divine Wisdom, please spare me

Why didn't I see this before I loved you?
Now I must make my bed and lie in it too
Only you, I think, could turn my love to my shame
So please, let me be a fool without saying her name

Apple and the Tree

Your poor mother
If she only knew
All of the shit
You put me through.

If she only knew that the pain
She felt from other men
Became the same pain
Dealt to me by her son.

You're more like your father
Than you think you are.

Not I

Was I not beautiful enough?
You were
Then was I not charming enough?
Now that's a laugh!
Was I too much?
No, my dear
Too frequent my touch?
Not at all
Is it because I would complain
When he hurt me again and again?
No, no, his fault was to hurt
Don't soil yourself with his dirt
It was not you,
It was him

But I tried my best all the time, I held down my needs
To avoid the fights, I ignored my boundaries
To see if it would work
I bruised my knees to please that jerk
So why her and not I?

I went to bed cold to please
I baked and cooked and packed to freeze
I danced I seduced I swirled I twirled
I took his "sorry"s about other girls
The benefit of doubt was overused
He convinced me it was lovemaking to be abused
So why her and not I?

I kept myself pretty all the time
I loved his family as if they were mine
I massaged, I doted, I smiled, listened, and laughed
Yet he blames it all on when my foot slammed down at last
Why did he make me feel I was asking too much?
There must be a reason it happened as such
So please tell me, why her, and not I?

It was not you, he knows that well
So he pulled you with him to the walls of hell
He is a man lost in his pain
Lost in his stubbornness, only himself to blame
He thought himself not good enough
He feared the pain so he acted tough
Don't get me wrong, he was selfish as well
And would not allow you to bid him farewell

Enough not a single woman will be
For he is not searching for a woman, you see
He's looking for himself, but he can't find him
Searches all the wrong places, 'til he can no longer swim
He is the very reason that he will drown
Let him not be the reason you wear that frown
Don't lose yourself in his grief
He knows you're too good, he couldn't let you leave
You point the finger in the wrong way
Your only fault is you let yourself stay

There will always be many hers with him
The her from the club, the her from before
The her from running, the her in his porn
But there's only one you and he knows what he's lost
Still he couldn't fix himself to avoid paying the cost

Normally to tango, it takes two
But it was all him, never you
Love yourself again,
For what I speak is true
You wasted your love trying to heal
A man whom in his pride,
Does not wish to be healed

It was all him
Not the hers
Nor even slightly you
And I hope he doesn't do this to the future thems too

Mirror

It's okay, there, there, I forgive you I do
You didn't hear me, didn't believe what was true
You treated me badly, put me in harm's way
Prioritized others, threw me to the fray
You gave away my love
Like it was cheap
Took nothing in return
Now I have nothing to keep

But I still love you, I do
You forget, but it's true
I forgive you my darling so wipe that tear
You've learned the lesson this time,
There's nothing left to fear

It's not your fault, you're not the one to blame
Just promise you won't let them hurt us again
All you did was love, like I love you
But don't forget, other me
We deserve love too

Wise

Do not ask for honey from he who makes only vinegar
When one wants honey, go only to a beekeeper

Whore

The woman is the whore, yet it's the man who thrusts
The woman is the whore, yet it's the man who persists
She is the whore, though she is pressured
She is the whore, though she is scared
She is the whore, though society tells her to comply for love
She is the whore, though society is telling her she must be a porn star for love
She is the whore, though her "no's" were disregarded
She is the whore, though she is cautious who she takes to bed
She is the whore, though she is the one that asks for protection
She is the whore, though she is the one who is ignored
She is the whore, though she is shamed for her sexuality
She is the whore, though he is the one that brags about how many he's bedded
She is the whore, though she turns her blame inwards
She is the whore, though he is the one that can't control himself
She is the whore, though in his fucking, she searches for signs of lovemaking
She is the whore, convincing herself of their love, while he thinks of his next whore
She is the whore, though she wishes only to have you
She is the whore, yet you still call her a prude
She is the whore, though you and society
Are the ones that ground her down, broke her,
Pressured her, shamed her, and trained her.
Yet, always, it will be she that is the whore
And never you

All Shots Fired

So, fuck you, truly
You're not my friend,
Get out of my face
I don't want to see you again

God bless the next woman
That has to deal with you
I'm sure she'll be smarter
Slam the door at the start
You're like a disease
That targets the heart

The best thing you did
Was walk away
You really disgust me
Get out of my face

It was me who stayed
I know I'm part to blame
But I can't stomach seeing you
All the same

I want to wipe out your existence
Not remember a thing
Erase the fondness
Until it's extinct

You can't love like this
Like the way that you are
You're a monster in the making
If you let yourself get that far

You feel no remorse,
Are you even aware
That you've become animalistic
Without an animal's instinct to care?

Burn

You don't have my heart
But a part of my soul
Not meaning that you deserve it
Nor that I gave it to you
Meaning that the void
In your heart is a dark pit
A vacuum
That has sucked the soul from me

Laura

He feeds the dog with the left
While petting the cat with the right
Then he sets them at each other
And stands back to let them fight

Quel Dommage

For it is a shame to burn the light,
The fire of a heart of innocence and love
By binding it with a heart that is a hole
Of darkness that only devours

When I Look At You

Part of me still loves you, of course
And I let her love you, I just tell her
To keep it hidden away
And I keep you far away
Because I think she loves an illusion of you
So I let her love the illusion
But it's dangerous to love the illusion of a man
When the reality of him is very different

Ghosts

Remembering is all I can do
To hear your laugh
To dance our dance
To smell your scent at the tip of my nose
To feel your hand
To hear your voice

Closing my eyes is the only way
To see you smile at me
To imagine it's you I'm kissing
That it's your body against my own
Your warmth heating me
Your shoulders under my hands

A memory is all I'm given
A memory is all I have
A memory that could've been every day
A memory you let slip away

A memory you refuse to forget
A memory you won't let me forget
And I refuse, too

Yes, the real you I've let go
Yes, I'll try to let in someone new
But the memories of us, my dear
Until the last moment
Those will I keep

Everything or Nothing?

You were everything I didn't want
That I tried to convince myself I wanted
Why? I still don't know
But I convinced myself well enough
That I thought I loved you
I let you in, I brought you home
Even though you were everything I didn't want
How? I still don't know
But the lie ate me up inside
I began to eat you up outside
I rebelled against the notion of us
While trying to solidify the notion of us
While trying to push you to be the man I wanted
But you were everything I didn't want
How did this happen? I do not know

#1

A finger strokes a cheek
A strand of hair slowly pulled aside
A tongue licks lips
Breath tickles a soft neck
A nipple turns hard
Whispers in an ear
The heat of another body
Lighting up your own
A candle glistens on wet skin
Eye contact held as lights switch off
Grazing lips slowly work their way up
To the top of a bare arm,
From the start of a delicate wrist
Fingertips trace the curves
Words we give grow us both
Our cheeks flood pink
Panting in unison intensifies
As moaning in unison flows
Depths of the soul are seen
As depths of the body explored

#2

He yanks your hair
You can't yank his
A red slap mark
Left on your face
Two hands tighten around your neck
Jaws break from shoving so deep
Someone touches you in your sleep
You're flipped around, so you can't see
As the fast pounding starts
Shoving mechanically
Stay quiet to "bitch, slut, whore"
A body is shoved on the floor
Bringing you lower than the words made you feel
The weight so heavy you cannot move
Hands held down, you're not free
Bruises on a body, your souvenir
Flipped over again, on your rear
Now on your knees as he stands
Something stings your eyes
And so ends this dance
If you're lucky
Then a cuddle you'll get
Which makes it pleasure
All in the end

#3

Tell me dear reader
From the two poems above
Which sounds like torture
And which sounds like love?
Which is erotica?
And which a horror story?
Which is pushed by society
Until you are blind and cannot see?
Which one is in your porn?
Which one is in your heart?
Use your brain and look at both
The time has come to be smart.

Don't let society lie to you
Heed this warning so you may see
Live love like poem number two
And it won't be long before it leaves you empty

Hunter and the Prey

How could I let this happen to me again?
I offered myself like a lamb for slaughter
I saw the pointed teeth of a predator
Yet I moved my hair and gave my neck willingly

I wish I could shake her and say:
My girl, that will not give you love.
But instead, I stood back
Watched her foolishly fall
Into the arms of a carnivore
Turn off her instincts, put her mind to sleep

She had time to flee
Yet I watched her ripped to shreds
Loving and giving as she bled

You amaze me still, other me
How you could see the light and love
In a man within whom there was no light to see

Title-less

The only passion I know now
Is hate

Wishes Come True

In the letter I once wrote you,
I said I wish I could say that I hate you,
Now I do
And I wish that I didn't
Because hate is a poison
That only poisons the one who drinks it

Who?

Who was the man
That I thought I loved?
Does he match the one
I think I hate?

Let Go

Don't let yourself be blinded by what you won't forget

White Walls

I miss you too much
I cannot find the words to say
How it felt to have someone else in me
That did not feel the same way

To have someone touch me
Who did not know where I liked to be touched
To have someone caress me
Who did not matter that much

It made me miss you
Though I thought I'd left you behind
In his arms I longed to kiss you
Though I wish you forever out of my mind

Oh lover, tell me
How did we go so wrong?
Yet when we were together
I imagined us so strong

And now we are nothing
And now here I am
Remembering you
In the arms of another man

Crazy

You called me crazy
In my anger at catching your lie
You called me crazy
When your coldness made me cry
You called me crazy
When I suspected what turned out to be true
You called me crazy
For standing up to you

You built the madness
You yourself with your own deeds
You met me closed
Convinced me it was safe to unfreeze
Once I opened
Then you had your fun
Now look upon
Everything that you've done

You want crazy?
Crazy you're about to see

On Second Thought

On second thought you're right
I won't take offense
Crazy is the only way to describe
What I've been since we commenced

Crazy when I trusted you
Crazy to let you in
Crazy to see your potential
Crazy to think you're the yang to my yin
Crazy to forgive
All those many, many lies
Crazy was not seeing
There is no soul inside

Crazy to stay
When I should've ran
But the height of my crazy
Was thinking you're a good man

Demona

I never knew how much fire
You lit in me
Until I saw the
F u r y
Painted in my words

Should the Lord have any mercy
He will spare you from seeing me again
You, who disgrace the name of all men

Broken Fairytale

Don't come near me ever again
Either my heart will once more melt
Tearing the scabs off old wounds
Or my eyes will see you clearly
And I would rather never know if
Under what I once saw as a prince
An ogre lurks instead

Fall

My downfall was my heart
Which I entrusted to you

Copy and Repeat

Why did it take us so long to be through?
You'll break the other women too
I really hope they have more common sense than me
Actually, it's not even common sense they need
It's a smaller heart, in fact
Because my heart led me to stay
Despite my head screaming
Run the hell away

No Shame

Too fast, to warm your bed
I'm not surprised
You match the stereotype
Of the weaker half of humanity
Or so their reputation
Seems to be
Hiding from emotions
By jumping to use another body

Was she sitting next to you
When you reached out to me?
Was she sleeping
When you used my pet name so sweetly?

Don't you dare do to her
What you did to me
My pain I will live with
But hers I will not
So I will block you
Until I'm forgot

Shadows

One of the greatest sorrows
That lingers and doesn't leave
Is that I was wrong about you

Emancipation

Our love needs masochism, you see
For only masochism would tolerate such depravity
But the problem is, my darling
I'm no masochist anymore
So here you go, you can walk
I've left you open the door

Confession

One thing I know for sure
Deep in my heart of hearts
If we were near each other when we ended
We would have never been able to be apart

Dreams

I cannot decide if at night
Right before sleep
Is the worst or best time

The worst because
It's when singlehood feels the most lonely
When words of comfort are sought
Where touch is missed
Where the mind starts to drift downwards
Into thoughts that stir carnally

Or is it the best?
Because in sleep I have a refuge
A safety net of dreams that I yearn for all day
With someone strong and safe and loving
By whose warm body I lay

Machine-Man

I have no pity for me
My whole pity goes to you
Though my heart was shattered
Wounded and scabbed
It's much stronger
Healthier than
The heart of yours
Which I see now is accursed

Less like a beating heart
More like a functional machine
Less like a living heart with emotions
More like a heart programmed only to pump blood

So, I bless you, old lover
May your cursed heart return
To the heart it was at birth

Toxic

Toxic
Doesn't begin to describe
The
Poison
You bring to someone's life

Shush

I lose a part of myself with
Every word that leaves your mouth
How they were lost in vain
The beatings of this heart

Can't Tell

I wrote so much hate
I wrote the monster side of you
I didn't hold back
He's a pervert, he's an ass
He's cold, doesn't feel
Only cares for himself
Doesn't know how to heal

Yet when the anger fades
You're my darling still
I see you have my heart
I worry you always will
The laughter and sex
Conversations and dreams
The travels and movies
And hiking the streams
The dancing, the cuddling
The twinkle in your eye
The heartache, the opening

Which one of you is the lie?

Blame

The tears in your eyes
When I said my goodbyes
After I dealt with too much
After hushed sentiments
And leaving your clutch
After a torturous ending, and a rougher start
Left me wondering in the end who was it
Who broke the other's heart?

Turning Tables

You miss me
And I miss you
Then why do we do this to each other?
Tell me, I beg of you

You yearn to write to me
And here I am dreaming of you
Yet I must shut you out,
And my own wants too

Then tell me, my dear,
Why torture us both?
Perhaps the masochist is you
And not I, as I once supposed

Take Me Dancing

The melodies haunt me
Wherever I go
From country to country
What are they trying to show?

You're the one who broke us
Why not follow you?
But the song follows me
Confusing false feelings with true

Song, ever-playing, I beg you to stop
As I move along, shop to shop
It's him, not me, you should follow
He caused the pain, too much to swallow

Yet your lyrics of dancing haunt me instead
Awakening the memories of when he twirled me to bed
Dancing and laughing, cheek to cheek
You cause me such sadness and make my day bleak

No more from you, I beg
This song is three years old!
Go haunt him in my stead
He is the one you should scold

Pop Rock Shrimp

Pop rock shrimp sits on my plate
Someone else ordered it
But I still see your face

Dynamite shrimp
They use here a different name
Same taste though
Same memories to shame

Fiery like our passion
Rocky like our love
Sent to remind us
From the gods above

Pop rock shrimp
You ordered all the time
When I was yours, my darling
And you were once mine

Dynamite shrimp
Who are you eating it with now?
I eat it with others
Yet you're still with me somehow

Pop rock shrimp we ate
Again and again
As I fell in love with you
Now nothing is the same

Except for pop rock shrimp
Doesn't change wherever I go
The name may change
But it's the same as it once was so

Flowing Words from a Torn Rose

Scared for myself, scared for my past
Scared for my sister, scared for my friends
Scared for the girl I once babysat
Scared for every woman I see
Tears well up, hollow and weak
wondering why I let you do those things to me

We disgraced lovemaking
We disgraced love
We disgraced union
We disgraced me

Scared
Scared and cold
Hoping to be told that
You see it now and you're not the same
You've changed your ways
And take responsibility for the breaking
Just like I take responsibility for letting you

I recall years ago
At the height of delusion
Not questioning what I was sold as lovemaking
Mistaking the toxic highs and lows
The survival instinct, adrenaline in my body
Coupled with the hormonal release of a hug
As pleasure and chemistry
But slowly and surely, my love of sex and of myself
Wilted like a rose picked by fingertips too roughened
That they are unable to feel the softness of petals below them
And so they seek only thorns

Picked and plucked
Until the wounded girl on the inside became more wounded
A decrepit shadow of her once luminescent self

You disgust me
But not as much as I disgust me

It's not consent when we're
Programmed to agree
Pressured to agree
Bullied to agree
Groomed to agree
When we're trying to normalize sexual abuse, assault
Harassment that we face on a daily basis
Trying to normalize and control how society makes us
Feel like whores and objects
And when you're older and more experienced and
We're looking to you for direction and safety and love

It's not pure consent because
It's not coming from a place of truth and safety
A place of self-awareness
Healing, discernment, and love

I wish I could say this to his face
See if he reacts like he is moved and cares
Or if he would turn to defend, become argumentative
Face a woman with tears in her eyes
Sharing raw feelings—inconvenient though they may be
With coldness and bullshit statistics, cherry picked
From the media backed by the industry of extortion and corruption

See if he reacts like a human, or a soulless machine

I wish more than ever I had an older
Wiser woman telling me:
No, that's not love
That's not normal
That's not healthy
You're not empowered
You're disempowered
You're doing it all in hopes of intimacy, protection, and love
Hoping to be picked when you are the one that should be picking
And at what cost?

You're breaking yourself
And you're doing it to normalize your past pains
Past violations
To normalize how society makes you feel
What society says you should do
And because you're told if you say no to these things
You're undesirable

I thought I was safe with you
Then I realized
I wasn't safe at all
I ended up getting hurt
Not emotionally or spiritually
Though certainly in that way, too
I'm talking physically

I wasn't safe.

You should've known better
But now I know
And No is a word that will leave my tongue
Like a sword

Little Girl

Little girl, stop crying
No one's coming to save you
Little girl, get up
Your lover won't come and save you
Little girl, wipe your tears
Your brother won't come and save you
Little girl, fix your hair
Your father won't come and save you
Little girl, straighten your dress
Your friend like a brother will not save you
No man young or old, blood or not
No man will keep you safe
No man will be your home
No man will heal you
No man will save you
Little girl, in that mirror
Who do you see?
Her, with the tears in her eyes
With the love in her heart
She looks broken now,
But the spirit of a warrior is in her
In that mirror, little girl
Is the one who will save you

Prize for Rotten Judgement

I think you're so special
And I thought he was too
Then I compare the poems
That I wrote him and I wrote you

Were either of you special then?
Or was I out of my mind both times?
Was the love real for either, all, or neither?
What was it I actually left behind?

Then I see I wrote nothing
For the one who loved me well
Though I send him love everyday
I start to wonder if I prefer your hell

What was it about the two of you
That really reeled me in?
What lapse in my sanity
What alluring call of sin?

What false promise of safety
That safe it made me not
What unspoken future
That I never even got

What large gestures of romance
That didn't really exist
What otherworldly doting
That with both of you I missed

My sanity must have left me
All those years ago
Because I chose the two of you to love
And why, I'll never know

Seeing it summed up
Now that my sanity is back
A message to end all messages
And perhaps one my other poems lack:

A lovely FU to you
And FU to you as well
I say goodbye to both of you
And so long to both your hells!

Une Mort Très Douce

I kept waiting for you to save me
And in my slow death
I learnt how to save myself

At Last, A Poem to the Highest Caliber of Man

My first love, my first love,
The love you gave me was unparalleled, the adoration unsurpassed
Equally matched only by the love I gave you
We poured equally into each other's cups
Never holding back, allowing truth and love to flow easily

You surprised me with letters and flowers all the time
Reminding me how grateful you were to be mine
You helped me, took care of me, and loved me well
And I took what you gave me and returned it tenfold:
Gifts and letters and songs and CDs
Clothes and cologne, and love decrees
Warm cooked meals and surprise dates
Our love was a love film
Fueling my belief in fairytales and fate

Though there were times you were lost, your soul was never lost
You knew who you were and what you stood for
You chose not to repeat the past of your father
You would adore and celebrate a woman
The way you wished someone would adore your sister and mother
You decided no person could lure you away from your love
Take you away from yourself and your principles
You understood it would destroy you as much as your lover

You honored my body with what you did to it
You were gentle and caring, and I recall when
Less experienced and younger, I came to you after reading
In the male-owned and dollar-bought magazines
That porn was an avenue for female sexual liberation
And echoed what I read: Should we watch it together?

"It's not for me," you said
"How can I watch what I know is fake?

When I know the women don't want to be there
They're just there getting paid?
Because they need the money
Or they are stuck or lost in life
Or trying to help their families
I can never enjoy it; it doesn't feel right."

...Oh, my old lover...
If you only knew, the barbarity of most men
When speaking of the same topic, so unlike you:
The lack of feeling, of right and wrong, of caring
The monkey brain they let lead them
How different they are to you!
Oh, how you were able to see with your heart and soul
To be led by compassion and love!

I met you so young and stayed with you so long
I assumed most men were like you
I would not even ask questions
Assuming simply that they, too
Had the same elements of your heart
Then I would discover far down the line
How broken, lost and unbalanced
Ungiving and selfish
Unprincipled and immoral
Disloyal and dishonest
Festering and unhinged
Taking and breaking
Too many were

When women tell me what they want in a partner, a lover, a divine union
When they share with me their fear that they will never meet men "like this"
Because men like this don't even exist
They think men like you are as real as Santa
A figment of the female collective's imagination

Besides thinking of other men whom I admire like you
I think of a man I had and gave myself to:
When I tell them about you, it's as if I'm telling them magic is real
Which by the way, I know it is.

When we parted I was like an innocent doe
Unaware of the lurking jackals and coyotes
Waiting around the corner
Unaware and trusting
Not waiting to see if I'm given to before I give
Ignorantly pouring and nurturing as much as I could with you
Unaware that I should not let them lead me down certain paths
Unaware that not all listen to "No"
That not all have your level of compassion,
Morals, principles and empathy
That not all think of women like you did
Like that day you showed me what you thought about porn

Unaware of what factors differentiated you from them
The biggest one I now see you shared with other great men:
A belief in and knowing a higher power
That something greater exists
That life and living and loving have purpose
Beyond what our shallow society's knowing insists
That we are souls, eternal beings in a physical body
This belief I've seen is one large decider
Between men like you and men like them:
The men like the ones this book is dedicated to

I was
Unaware
That when a jackal smiles at a doe
He bares his teeth not because he is happy to see her
But because he is preparing to devour her

I have learnt now just how much of a gem you were
Even more of an admirable man
I bless you truly every day
Send you good wishes whenever I can
These other men: richer, taller, or more handsome
More experienced, more confident, more strong
More well-travelled, better dancers, better spoken
Better actors, better fakers
More adventurous, more wild

Regardless of all of that
As men
As souls
They do not come even close
To being the caliber of human you are

They cannot even touch
The level of your feet
The light of their soul
Is like the stench of garbage
When compared to the golden glow
Coming from a heart
As good and pure as yours

I pity the women they will have next
I know the pain these women will feel
I send them prayers, for the safety of their hearts
Their innocence and souls
But your current love
I know she's in good, safe hands
She might not know, but I know, how lucky she is
To be with the highest caliber of man

Seduced by the Devil

I didn't see you coming
Distracted by my last lover's hurt
Frozen by his roughness
My aloofness was your challenge to convert

Despite your gifts, and planning of trips
Despite your crazy, over-the-top gestures
And your perfectly sculpted lips
I still didn't see you coming

Then somewhere in between all your lovely words
Between your arrogant cockiness
And months of promises which seemed absurd
I was surprised when something in me stirred again

At the sound of your deep voice
Like a fly to a Venus fly trap
Like a snake seduced by a charmer
Your honey called me in
Seduced by the devil
And foreign thoughts of sin

But this time my instinct saved me
From what? I'll never know
I listened when a voice said walk away
Something dark stirred in your handsome eyes
And finally healed, I knew this time not to play

Yet thoughts of you still sometimes creep into my mind
And I wonder how someone with whom I've never shared a bed
Can return lost carnal desires for me to re-find
After living through my last lover made me think they were forever dead

And For God's Sake, Walk Her to Her Car

A man stood at my window
When I was all alone
He watched me from my window
I was the only one home

My instincts screamed danger
Before I turned and saw his face
My window was open, you see
The feeble mesh between us my only saving grace

I'll spare you the details of the story
How he spoke to me with words like "sexy" and tried to come in
Because I came out well
And am still living in this skin

But after, the fact that he watched me from my window
I couldn't get out of my head
Had the story ended differently
Would I have been left for worse than dead?

I was reminded quite quickly
Why being female, single, and alone was a risk
How in a second my life and body were in danger
For having the window open alone at half past six
How none of this would've happened
If my last lover was still by my side.

Would I trade to receive his form of torture,
Would I tie myself to him again,
Just to be able to exist in my home knowing
That a man would not try to get in?

I'd be able to go on my travels
Without being followed nonstop
I'd be able to walk freely
Without being whistled at, or hiding in a shop

I wouldn't have to plan my day around
Being back by the setting of the sun
I could enjoy the night sky for once, without wanting to run
Or enjoy the peace of nature in isolation; a luxury;
For only a suicidal woman hikes alone, believe you me

I could go to an isolated beach
I could sleep on an overnight train
I wouldn't have to walk clutching my key
I could listen to my music in a taxi ride
I wouldn't need to scan my Airbnb
For an emergency place to hide
I could crack open the window
On a hot summer night
I could sleep a whole night without waking
To the sound of the slightest creak
I could accept a drink as an offering
Or even enjoy more than one drink in a day
I could live my daily life knowing
I was not some stranger's prey

That group of men that blocked my way when I refused to give my number
Wouldn't have existed
The hotel manager that kept showing up to my room door
Wouldn't have persisted
The man that blocked me on the street and touched me
Wouldn't have dared
The taxi driver that tried to kidnap me
Would've been too scared
The new male friend who crossed the boundary unwarranted in his car
Wouldn't have tried
Had I only stayed with my broken human of an ex...
But my soul would have died inside

Strength and independence
Resilience and bravery
I know very well
I have more than most men

But
The predator with his hand towards me at my window
Made me realize
It may not matter how strong inside I am
Because sadly in this world
I will always indeed *need* a man
Yet I will never accept just *any*

The cost of a woman waiting for the right one
You can read in my list above
And I will pay it over again
To not live a deformed version of love

Once upon a time,
I exchanged my sanity for a feeling of protection
Never more will I repeat that mistake.

The next time you see a woman
Living her single life independently alone
I hope you see the strength inside of her
Whereas otherwise you might've never known

Absolutes

"No absolutes, oh no, not for me,"
You insisted again and again
No "forever," "never," "always"
Speaking words of a future you can't comprehend

Yet when my eyes last laid on yours
Your tears reflected in my own
I asked you for a promise and you gave it to me
To never leave me for more than a month alone

"I promise, never, never again,"
Were your words, my dear
The last I checked "never" was an absolute
The very thing you most fear

The saddest part of all
Is the "never" came in a different way
We never saw each other again
Our goodbyes we didn't even get to say

Never again did our arms wrap around each other
Our heads tucked neck-to-neck
Never again our bodies intertwined with one another
Never your presence next to me to protect

Never again hearing
Your voice pant in my ear
Never again your calmness
Rationalizing away my fears

Never your cheek against mine
As we twirled and swayed side-to-side
Never your warm arms
Giving me a safe place to hide

Nevermore the candlelit dinners
A disguise for our battles of wit
Never again to touch that hand
Which in mine so perfectly fit

Never to have your fingers
Run through my strands of hair
Never another adventure
No more new memories to share

No more the long nights of dancing
Nor the movies from my favorite spot on your legs
Nor your unique brand of romancing
Left on my car or in little chocolate eggs

This was not what I wanted
When I asked you for absolutes
But an absolute you still gave me
This fact I can't refute

You see, absolutes came regardless
They're in fact an unavoidable way of life
But the direction that they come in, my darling
Only you get to be the one to decide

Wolf in Sheep's Clothing

I saw a picture of my smile
Before you broke it.

In the image
Innocence and happiness shone through
I could feel the light
Before you took it

I remember I had just met you
After the year I had, you felt different
The way you sold yourself; different
But I see now you were the same
Just a wolf in sheep's clothing

Dangerous. More dangerous than the last
Worsening the trauma from the past
Appearing innocent and doe-eyed like a lamb
Sneaking and crushing until your victim is damned

Question

One last question
For you from me
Can either of us
Really ever be free?

From Comrade to Foe

I viewed you as my protector
You're not my protector
You were never my protector
You were my destroyer

I see now that the truth was
I needed someone to protect me from you

Karma is a Poet

It's time you learnt
Your deeds have consequences
And I shall be your teacher

It's time you finally
Reap what you sow
Allow me to lift up the scythe
To help you

It's time you paid
For the pain you caused others
I will speak
For your past lovers that did not

Your lack of caring, lack of accountability
It cannot go unpunished

Your darkness has spread
It awoke a demon in me
She says hello to you
And told me to relay
A message she has for you:

I,

I am your reckoning.

Enough Crying

You did nothing wrong
You did nothing wrong
You did nothing wrong
You did nothing wrong

I'm sorry those you tried to turn to first
Made you feel otherwise
I'm sorry you believed them and gaslighted yourself

What you did during survival mode
During that lie and after

Was not you

None of them can take your integrity from you

You did not deserve what happened
You did not deserve the aftermath

What you did in your wilted hypnotic slumber
In the limbo of your existence
Before you opened your eyes
Was not you

You did nothing wrong

You did nothing wrong

You did nothing wrong.

Mea Culpa

I forgive you
I forgive you for it all
I know it was not in your heart
I've forgiven you from the very start
I forgive you again, my dear
I forgive you, have no fear
I forgive you and I wish you love
I know our breaking was very rough
It broke me more than you could know
Forgive me for the anger that I should have let flow
But that instead festered inside
And came out when there was nowhere else to hide
It came out fiercely in my words
But I'm a writer, I know the magic of words
Everything we've done is gone and in the past
And now it's time to turn the page at last
And though I won't talk to you
And you don't know why
It's because done is done
And it's time to say goodbye
Perhaps in another life you and I will meet again
But now so long forever, my lover, my darling, my friend

Regaining Innocence: The Only Truth

Those who have felt love have known God
It is the purest thing on the planet
Those who can relish in it
Without fear, without shame
Are relishing in pure happiness
Those who can give it,
Without fear, without shame
Are spreading the sole gift of
Mankind that makes us
Redeemable

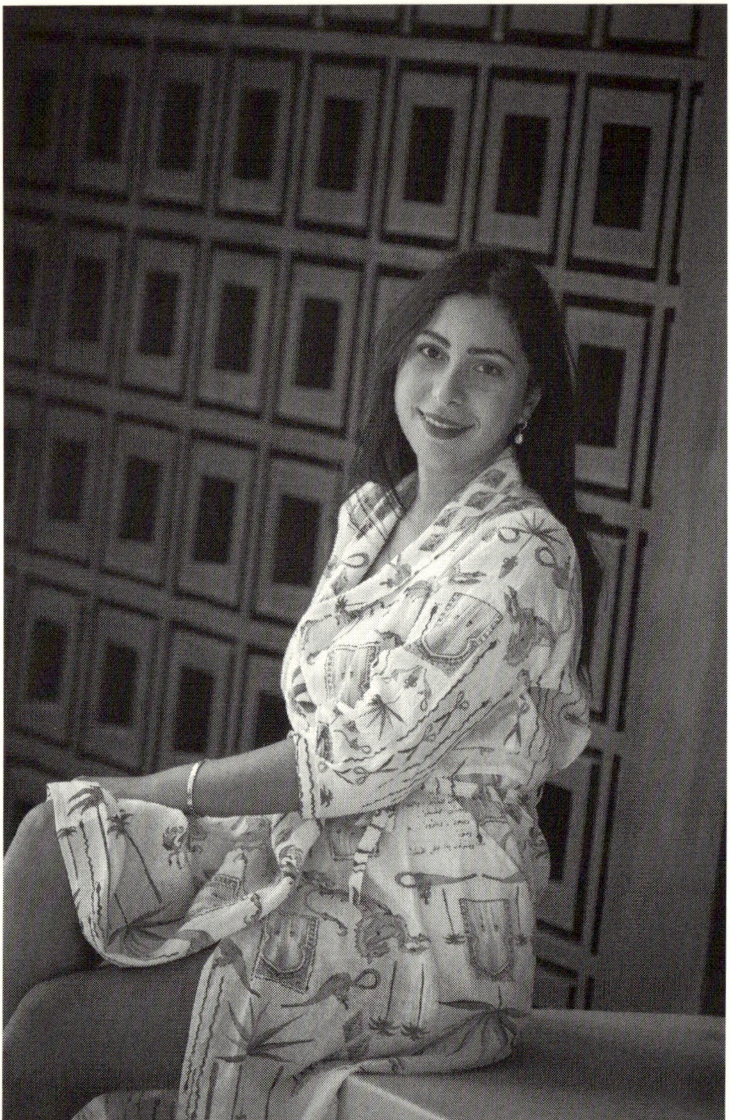

ABOUT THE AUTHOR

Petra Mourany was born in the freezing flatlands of Ohio to loving immigrant parents originally from the Eastern Mediterranean. Almost immediately after her birth, her parents moved to the newly developing United Arab Emirates, where she spent her whole pre-university life raised as an expat going to an international British school. After returning to the freezing flatlands for university, she found herself on the West Coast of the US, working for big-name tech companies—some that rhyme with "frugal" and "top hat"—in sunny, spiritual-friendly and acai-bowl filled Los Angeles for a few years. Finally, passion overtook logic, and she quit her job to start her own life-coaching practice, and to dedicate more time to writing allegorical fantasy novels, various nonfiction, and the type of controversial poetry that would make most Middle Eastern parents gasp.

Pulled away from writing or coaching, you'll likely find her at a beach, your nearest bachata club, or making a green smoothie while daydreaming about finally owning a large black Great Dane, a German Shepherd, and a little Cavalier King Charles Spaniel.

To keep up to date with Petra, go to *www.petramourany.com* for more info!

Made in the USA
Middletown, DE
21 February 2022